What Happens When the Night Falls

Roog Kubur

BookLeaf Publishing

India | USA | UK

What Happens When the Night Falls © 2022
Roog Kubur

All rights reserved.

No part of this publication may be
reproduced, stored in a retrieval system, or
transmitted, in any form or by any means,
electronic, mechanical, photocopying,
recording or otherwise, without the prior
written permission of the presenters.

Roog Kubur asserts the moral right to be
identified as author of this work.

Presentation by *BookLeaf Publishing*

Web: www.bookleafpub.com

E-mail: info@bookleafpub.com

ISBN: 978-93-5744-893-2

First edition 2022

ACKNOWLEDGEMENT

Thank you to every English teacher who suggested writing as something I was actually good at. Thank you to my mentors for helping me find my voice after so long. Thank you to my parents for never stopping me along that discovery. Thank you to my sister for making me feel like it was okay to take my time. And thank you to my friends, despite never knowing what I'm up to.

PREFACE

What happens when the Night falls? The Day breaks.

The Vagabond.

People keep asking "who are you?"
As if I have an answer.

I've been through the darkest reaches,
of my mind, of my body, of something,
to bring to light just a sliver of myself.

But alas, here I sit
another roadside attraction
a frozen image of what once was
for passerbys to gawk,
widen awe-struck eyes,
and grant precious pity to.
Staring at the broken pieces
of a mirror image.

I lost myself
this time last year.
I stopped looking at
who I knew, where I was, what I saw,
and forgot how quickly the world
moves without mercy.
I got caught in the crossfire
of idolizing the images in my mind
and going back to once was.

(I didn't make it out alive.)

So I try desperately to catch back up
but between courtesy calls and busy break work
It becomes another image to chase.
The world will keep moving forward,
and I will always remain
three
steps
behind.

Look Up In The Sky!

The stars have learned to hide their shine
to protect against greedy eyes
looking to commodify, commercialize, colonize
what they have to offer.
So the sky remains its brilliant midnight
deeper than the hurting souls occupying her
time,
vaster than the reaches of what we understand,
brighter than our greatest minds.
(Once you look past the greying smoke of
indoor fires,
of course.)

The moon, however, stands her ground,
giving guidance to weary travellers and
wandering eyes,
who's broken spirits make her cry.
But only a fool would trust her spotlight in the
sky.
For just when you think you've found your way
home,
she's gone, like a thief of your time.

"I'll be back soon," she says with warm eyes and
a smile,
Knowing damn well we'll be right back where
we started.

The Silence of the City

What a tired image.
Just outside the warmth of His love,
guarded closely by stone walls and wooden
gates
and metal fences with sharpened tips,
opening only to safeguard, protect, and save
those
who have been cast aside,
who's paths have led them astray,
who need a place,
lie people.

Bodies deemed unworthy,
unseemly, unlovable, unfixable,
worthy of nothing more than pity,
even less than the change in your pocket.

A skillful detour prevents this image:
Avoid street corners, building nooks,
underpasses of bridges, train stations,
and the riverside.
Better yet, avert your gaze all together

To maintain pity as humanity.

La Vie En Rose

I live in a second reality
where I've deluded myself into thinking
that these journeys with no destination
would eventually come to an end

That I, like Sisyphus,
could muster all my strength
to keep moving forward
and find something new.

The tango I do every night
without variation
the jazz number
without modulation
the motions of the play,
where I, the player, catch every beat
the unrehearsed symphony
that sounds the same.

This reality brings comfort,
the promise of another day,
where something happens
to make this dance, this number, this piece, this
song
worthwhile.

La Vie En Rouge

I live in a second reality
Where I've accepted that this world
will change.
And this inevitable change
will bring humanly salvation
to save us from ourselves.

That I, like Atlas,
could muster all my strength
to save and solve the chaos and strife
with love and compassion.
That the giants atop the hill
will one day become our friends
and carry us out
of the blackened pit below
by way of some unnamed magician.

But alas, in the common sense reality
I see visions of hopelessness
masquerading as intelligence.

A denial of delusions
in favour of pumping green
through eroded pipes

by way of time travel
to return us to salvation.

9

Each Tick of A Clock

Time passes. It has to.
Because otherwise each tick of a clock
is rendered useless,
and each phase of the moon, earth, and sun
are nothing more than movements,
and each night
is indefinite.

Because the differentiation of these things
marked by "each"
is otherwise meaningless, excessive verbiage
grasping at meaning.

But that doesn't stop each night
from suffocating her prey
in an interminable loop
every time they come.

The midnight blackness looks the same
whether three, four, five minutes or hours pass.
No matter how tight I squint or how far my neck
cranes

tomorrow is just out of reach.

I've become more convinced
that the passage of time is inevitable
Because otherwise the tick of a clock
is a reminder of my fate
and the phases of the moon, earth, and sun
are markers of madness
and the night
laughs in my face.

Tales of Children Born from Nothing

A radical food for thought:
Children born from nothing
That somehow know everything
Desperate to keep anything
From becoming something.

These children have seen a world unlike yours
And know what exists beyond it.
They mock you for your ignorance
Then boast their false pretences.

These children live in a world unlike yours
skillful cartographers of the new world
while simultaneously constructing another
demolishing what came before it.

These children know naught of your love
For they have never seen it before
They replace it with knowledge
Of the next big thing.

These children born from nothing

know better than to expect something
From a low life anything
Making green from everything.

What Does It Take?

What does it take to be a poet?
Wit. Entitlement. Greed.

Tell the story you want to tell.
Make it your own or make it engaging.
Convince the reader your work is worth reading
Convince yourself your work is worth writing.

Dance with your reader.
Always stay 2 lines ahead & 2 steps behind.
Throw in red herrings to make them feel smart.
Throw in red herrings to add colour to black
words.

Expect them to understand.
Keep your words fluid & stance firm.
Tell them the story they want to hear,
Tell them the story they need to hear.

Make your poetry your own.
Nevermind the shared stories you tell.
Make a poem relatable enough to be shared,
Make a poem relatable enough to be stolen.

Lie your way through the piece
To reveal your true intentions.

Use overused metaphors
To convey new meaning.

Verbose diction is your only tool
To ensure your message is clear.

Write in lines on empty pages
To evoke chaos in your thinking.

But most important of all:
Understand your work is the best.
Because all poets are liars
disguised as artists.

Fire In The Night

I'm tired of the fire burning within me.
It consumed my lungs, my heart, my soul
Dried up all my rivers and lakes
Boiled my blood to suffocation
And continues to char my blackened bones.

My mind has not seen peace
Since the day they lit the match
And fed me fuel disguised as food
To calm my aching stomach
Hungry for peace.

My eyes remain dry.
I no longer cry tears for those lost
But instead must avenge
Cursing the carelessness of the people
That dare rest in the face of danger.

I no longer dream in my sleep
But fantasize
of a world beyond my fire
Reaching out to this far away place
Until the mirage succumbs to my flame.

The world is a permanent red.
My skin is forever hot.
My mind has turned to ash.
The sun never sets
in this empire of my last breath.

It's Hard To Be An Optimist

I prefer to look at the world
I tend to notice glaring flaws behind glaring
lenses
Preferring to watch the tired eyes
from 40 hour minimum wage shifts.

I don't fantasize about blue skies and sunshine
cause when I look down all I see is burning
smoke.
I don't protest my government
because it was my choice.

I'd rather criticize the actions of others
Than focus on the good traits
Because it's hard to see the good
When it is clouded behind the worst.

Optimism is a buzzword meaning be happy.
But how can I be happy when I know the truth
That I'm not the same as everyone I meet
That hope ultimately ends in another goal to
meet?

It's hard to be an optimist
cause I'm more of a realist
And the reality is
That optimism feels like bullshit.

To My Dearest:

How can I find the beauty when the world's
become so ugly?
When passion became a cliche and
cringeworthy?
When all artists live hidden away out of fear of
money?
When "art" became synonymous with
"pretentious"?
How do I write you my love when my love has
become scarce?
I used to give my heart to the world in pieces:
A piece to the thunderous mountain with still
rivers and grey clouds,
Another to these dark night skies lit by
disappearing stars behind city skylines,
And one to the warmth of my home filled with
enticing aromas.
How can I hide my affection?
How?

Dividing the Sky

What happens when you divide the sky?
Who decides who gets what?
Where are the lines drawn?
When will we start?

Who gets the eastern sky?
When the sun rises each day,
When we begin our lives,
When we meet a new face?

Who gets the southern sky?
When we meet our first days,
When we make our own ways,
When we build our own mistakes?

Who gets the western sky?
When we live not for ourselves,
When we hold out helping hands,
When we guide instead of stray?

Who gets the northern sky?
When we've lived through our mistakes,
When we remember old names,
When we have lived our days?

Dividing the Land

What happens when we divide the land?
Who belongs where?
Where do we go?
When will we decide
Why we've divided the sky?

Who gets the eastern land?
Where the sea meets the eye,
Where visitors make new homes,
Where we meet a new face?

Who gets the southern land?
Where we work our first days,
Where we are taught the right way,
Where we build the paths?

Who gets the western land?
Where we count our everything,
Where we live for ourselves,
Where we've made our own ways?

Who gets the northern land?
Where the nights become longer,
Where we've forgotten our names,
Where we've lived our final days?

The Purity of Water

Let the water come down to soothe our pain,
To clean our lungs from the rising dust,
To bring a cool hand upon our warmed skin,
to fill our empty cups.

Let it trickle down, down, down,
all through the silent night.
Let it fill our ears with her soft pitter patter.
Let her sing her deceiving calm.

Until we wake and the soft pitter patter hasn't
ceased.
She continues to sing throughout the day.
The never ending pitter patter pitter patter pitter
patter drives you mad.
All thoughts hidden behind the soft pitter patter
pitter patter pitter patter,
Until all you hear is the soft pitter patter pitter
patter pitter patter of the falling sky/
Absorbing every part of your fractured mind
until you step outside.

The soft pitter patter is now sheets falling to the
blackened ground.

She no longer cools your burning skin but it
burns to feel the cool slaps against your skin,
beating you back inside.

But back inside the pitter patter persists until she
found her next victim.
her crystal blue turned muddy brown,
living above the unstable streets,
building walls so you can't escape,
confined to a breaking home.
Falling apart when the pitter patter seeps into the
vulnerable cracks,
Breaking piece by piece until all you have is the
pitter patter.
Nowhere to go and nowhere to hide from the
uniform pitter patter pitter patter pitter patter
All you have is the persistent pitter patter pitter
patter pitter pitter patter.

May she sing her song to empty crowded streets,
to rebuild our broken homes,
to drive us all, absolutely, positively, insane.

The Absence of Thinking

What happens when there's no one.
No one telling you how to act, how to think,
how to feel.
I'm constantly complaining of the cacophony of
voices telling how to walk, talk, sit, stand but
now.
Now they've stopped.
My mind has become a chalice run dry with
dissatisfaction
and the insatiable thirst for living
has disappeared.

I now echo reality (the scariest part of living).
I can no longer filter what happens, oh no.
What happens manifests in my mind and sits
there
until I am topped up with another dose of reality.
The reality that I am not who I say I am.
The reality that I'm nothing without the voices,
lying
convincing me I'm worth the time.

The reality that living in this reality without the
luxury of thinking
is the worst way to live.

I've convinced these voices to leave,
but that was the worst decision I've ever made.
And now, I stand,
with sweaty palms, shaky legs, and scanning
eyes,
disguising my trembling voice
because the only drop that managed to remain in
my empty cup
was the constant reminder:
Hide your feelings in cheap metaphors
and empty words.

A Love Poem

I won't write you a love poem.
I won't waste my precious words and strokes of
my pen on the way you took my breath away.
Or how you managed to entangle my every
thought.
How my words come out flowery and frivolous
when I describe your being
How I think in metaphors to compare how you
made me feel.

I know now the feeling is incomparable,
inescapable.
I will no longer shed burning tears from stinging
eyes turned red with rage.
I used to feel butterflies up to my throat at the
thought of being near you.
Cloudy minds with words unsaid of how you to
make you like me.
A most impossible event.

I will live in forever heartbreak knowing I'm not.
I'm not.

I'm not a poet,
so I won't write you a love poem.

I'm simply broken with thoughts entangled by
you.
With pen strokes on a blank page
of how much I hate you.

A Spitting Image

You spend so long looking at distorted images
that you begin to think them real.

Each window pane offers a distorted image.
Sometimes details are gone,
imitating nuance,
leaving fuzzy facial images behind.
Sometimes shapes are broken,
revealing importance.
But sometimes,
(sometimes)
You stare back.
A perfect mirror image
distorted by self-perception.

I Dreamed of A King

The king sat mighty,
Perched atop his pearlescent throne
The kingdom was at peace,
A moment of solace against the death and
demise.
The crown was where it was meant to be,
Atop, proudly, the head of the king.

The blue sky then filled with smoke
At the arrival of a young woman.
Beautiful, young, wise.
Bringing with her clarity,
Hidden among the grey clouds.

The smoke soon turned to soot
Blackening the air we once breathed
Filling our lungs with black.
Black.
We no longer belong to the kingdom,
We belong beyond.

The king, high and mighty,
Must protect his people right?
Save us from the dark,
We now fear.

The woman, clear and wise,
Will protect our people.
She will save us from the dark,
We now embrace.

The king, non violent and clever,
Will use his wit to save us.
No need to draw
When we have words
Mighty as he.

The woman, smart and resourceful,
Will use her wit to save herself
Accuses without words,
For she has wit,
Stronger than he

The king, scared and afraid,
Asks why she must seal his fate.
No longer wanting to fight,
Drops his sword.

The woman, defiant and proud,
Stands her ground

And fights as a king.

The people, now darkened and afraid,
See their king,
Facing a coward.

The people betrayed and hurt,
Embrace the darkness.
Long live the king.

Rotting Flowers Smell of Sweet Honey

Rotting flowers smell of sweet honey
And harbour beating hearts with broken parts
To rebuild bloody starts.
But a scent so sweet could only satisfy
departed eyes & undermine pregnant minds
desperate to return to their hives.

You & I alike see the scent of
deception, wilted beyond comprehension.
This wicked thing cries for forgiveness
Apologizes for its selfish, vicious
illness promising to deliver us that delicious
sweet, sickly honey.

But that same quickness brings us
a decision. Rotting flowers smell of sweet honey
but sweet honey tastes of deep amber.

When The Sun Looks Her Best

The sun looks best
when unobstructed by cooling clouds of grey
when blanketed by a brilliant sky so great,
when stared at blankly.
Not staring at remnants of her memory
or feeling her warm embrace
or remembering where she once was.

The sun looks best at night
when her brilliance is reflected
turning into a friendly spotlight
when she no longer intimidates
but brings something less sinister.
The sun looks best
when dancing in the moonlight.

Reintroductions.

I cannot continue on without the reintroduction
and destruction of my former self.

I've spent so long trying to be,
the older, better version of me
Trying to live up to the creation
of who I was in my own mind
Trying to go back to who I was
before these endless nights.
They tore down what I thought
were the core parts of my identity
and left dust in its place.

They created cracks
in my ever-breaking self,
withering away my soulless smiles
until my face was all I had left of me.

My iridescent sorrows skillfully hidden
by my insatiable desire to go back,
but who was I before these nights?
Was I who I thought I was,
or was it another reality for comfort?

Living on, pretending to know
feels wrong in my heart.
But living on, with everything up to destiny,
feels even worse.

Allow me the pleasure of reintroducing myself:
I am not a victim of the night.
I am a vagabond.
I am the product of conflicting ideas.
I am the very thing
preventing my own destruction.
I am a child born from nothing,
comprised of everything.

I don't know what I am
but a simple man
on the indefinite, fruitless search
for who I thought I was.

www.ingramcontent.com/pod-product-compliance
Lightning Source LLC
La Vergne TN
LVHW010924200726
843509LV00013B/2063